All Aboard The Toy Train

Compiled by Tony Bradman

Illustrated by Ian Cunliffe

HODDER
Wayland

an imprint of Hodder Children's Books

It's Got to Have Wheels!

It's got to have wheels,
It's just got to have wheels.
If you're getting me a present
Then it's got to have wheels!

Want to push it,
 Want to park it,
  Want to skid it round the carpet.
   Want to rev it,
    Want to race it,
     Want to send it off and chase it.

Don't want anything that's cuddly,
 That speaks, or squeaks, or squeals.
  If you're getting me a present
   Then it's got to have wheels!

Give me wheels, wheels, wheels,
 Only wheels, wheels, wheels.
  If you're getting me a present
   Then it's got to have wheels!

So please, please remember:
I just
 Want
  Wheels.

Paul Bright

Racing Cars

Engines roaring,
tyres squealing.
Formula One –
fantastic feeling.

Overtaking!
Fight for lead.
Flashing past –
amazing speed.

Accelerating
into curve.
Can they do it?
Will they swerve?

In a spin,
watch them roll.
Racing cars
out of control.

What a crash!
Who survived?
Toy cars dented –
we're alive.

Jane Clarke

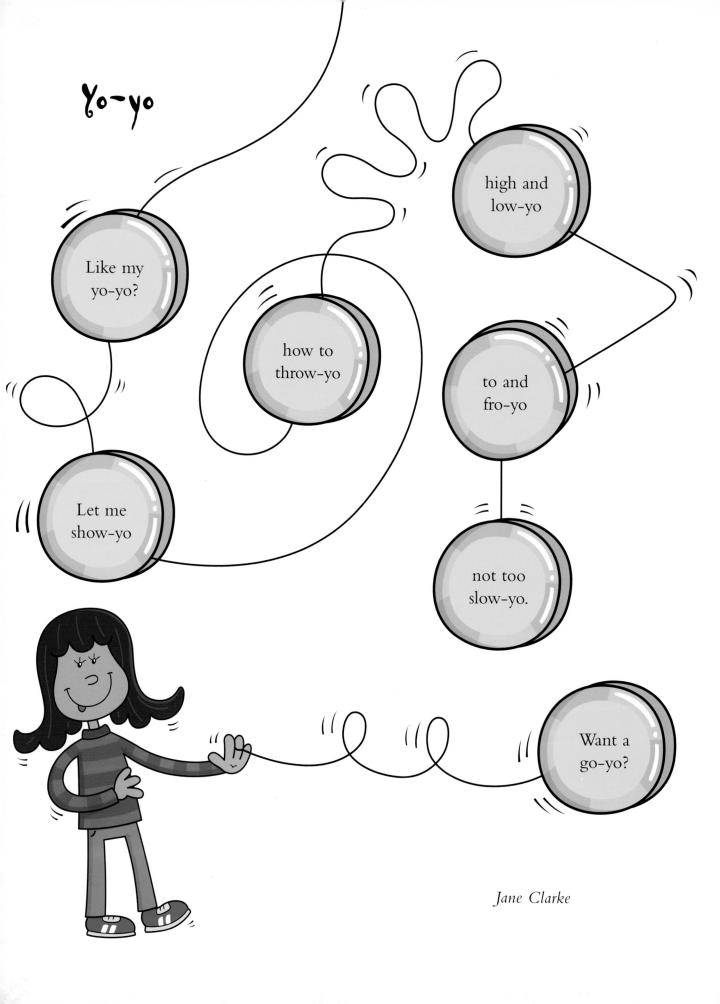

Rocking-horse Rider

When life is so awful I just want to scream
I ride on my rocking-horse into a dream.

I'm a Samurai swordsman
Who fights with a frown,
A cavalry captain
Who storms up and down.

I'm a hero who chases
The dragon from town,
A Robin Hood outlaw
Who pounds up and down.

I'm a knight dressed in silver,
A king with a crown,
A galloping jockey
Who leaps up and down.

I sing like a cowboy,
I smile like a clown,
I spring from my horse,
Tie him up, brush him down.

But when I'm asleep and the stars softly gleam
I ride on my rocking-horse into a dream.

Clare Bevan

Sofa Boat

Sofa boat, sofa boat,
bobbing on the sea,
take me to an island
with a coconut tree.

Sofa boat, sofa boat,
riding through the gale,
I'll steer you into harbour
and mend your tattered sail.

Sofa boat, sofa boat,
anchored in the night,
rock me gently as I sleep
until the morning light.

Sofa boat, sofa boat,
sailing in the sun,
float me softly on the waves
until the day is done.

Sofa boat, sofa boat,
bobbing on the sea,
take me on a journey
then bring me back for tea.

Tony Mitton

Oh, Dear, What Can the Matter Be?
(A nearly true story)

Oh, dear, what can the matter be?
Polly, my dolly, got flushed down the lavatory
I forgot to hold on to her nappy
While washing her bonny brown hair.

She slid down the pan and she shot round the U-bend
She whooshed through the pipework and out at the far end
She popped up at Putney and headed for Southend
With weeds in her bonny brown hair.

Mum's promised to buy me a dolly called Dotty
With tresses and dresses all stripy and spotty
Who wriggles and giggles and sits on the potty
And doesn't have horrid brown hair.

Oh, dear, what can the matter be?
I got a note from a lady in Battersea
Polly was found in the Thames there last Saturday
Mud in her bonny brown hair.

Jan Burchett and Sara Vogler

My Sea

I caught the sea in my bucket
to take it home with me
a shiny pebble shimmered
and drifted in my sea.

I caught the sea in my bucket
to take it home with me
a tiny winkle snorkelled
and drifted in my sea.

I caught the sea in my bucket
to take it home with me
a darting fish of silver
drifted in my sea.

Aivlys L. Hardy

Cyber (BLEEP!) Message

Urgent message	BLEEP!
From your cyber-pet	
Battery low	BLEEP!
Burn-out threat	
Must have volts	BLEEP!
Did you forget	
To press the button	BLEEP!
Marked RESET?	
Hurry, hurry	BLEEP! BLEEP! BLEEP!
I'm upset	
If I was flesh	BLEEP!
I'd shake and sweat	
Power fading	BLEEP!
Now I bet	
You'll have to call	BLEEEEEEEEEP!
The cyber-vet	
You'll find her on	BLEEP!
The Internet	

Tony Bradman

Naughty Doll

She says I never eat my dinner up.
She calls me, "naughty", throws me on the floor.
"If you're not good," she scolds, "you'll get a slap.
I've told you a thousand, million times before."
She says I never stay still where I'm put.
It's not my fault. It's just the way I'm made.
I'm not like other dolls. I flop about.
I'll never be a soldier on parade.

When Teddy, China Doll and me play school
I'm always doing things I shouldn't do.
She screams at me and calls me, "stupid doll",
Because I can't remember two plus two.
It's not my fault. My head is full of stuffing.
I'm rags and patches. Got a nothing nose.
Take one look at me, you'll burst out laughing.
Made in too much of a hurry, I suppose.

I've got no neck. My hair's a woolly mess.
One arm's too short, the other much too long.
My ears don't match. My eyes don't fit my face.
And all the different bits of me look wrong.
China Doll's pretty. Teddy's got soft fur.
But I don't mind. Despite her shouts and screams
I'm still the one she takes to bed with her
To keep the dark out and to share her dreams.

Leon Rosselson

Let Me Have a Go!

I've got this kite
A stunter, right?
And the breeze is beginning to grow
So when Dad's got it assembled
Then he'll let me have a go

It's the brightest green
You've ever seen
With a luminous sort of glow
And when Dad's checked it works OK
He'll let me have a go

You can dive it, turn it
Once you learn it
Weave it to and fro
Dad's checking there's not too much wind
And then I'll have a go

You can loop it around
Skim it on the ground
It's easy once you know
I think Dad's got the hang of it
So it's time I had a go

Nice figure-of-eight
But it's getting late
I really think... Oh, no!
Dad's only gone and crashed it
And I never had a go!

Paul Bright

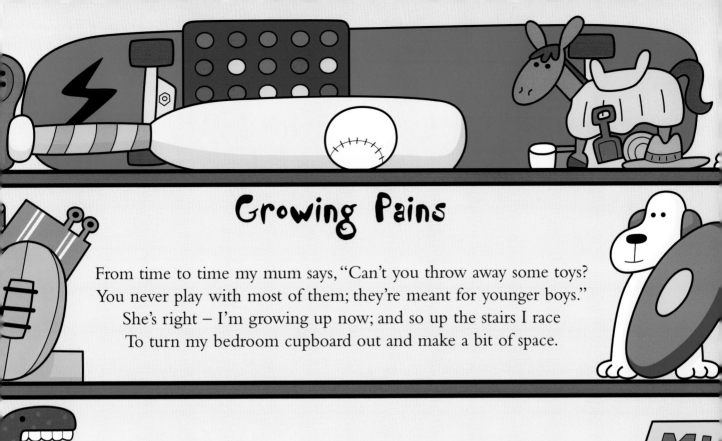

Growing Pains

From time to time my mum says, "Can't you throw away some toys?
You never play with most of them; they're meant for younger boys."
She's right – I'm growing up now; and so up the stairs I race
To turn my bedroom cupboard out and make a bit of space.

And then I face the tricky bit (and every year's the same).
I want to keep the soldiers, and that silly murder game.
The Lego set is handy on a dreary rainy day,
And, yes, I love my Teddy bear – so Teddy's going to stay.

The Rollerblades are precious (I must fix the wheel that sticks);
I couldn't chuck my magic kit before I've learnt the tricks.
My train set's well worth keeping, though it's missing half its track.
So, once again, I chicken out and shove the whole lot back.

John Yeoman

What I Wanted

At the age of ONE
A rattle to shake and chew upon

At the age of TWO
A teddy bear, faithful and true

At the age of THREE
A tricycle as new as can be

At the age of FOUR
A fearsome, gruesome dinosaur

At the age of FIVE
A silver kite to swoop and dive

At the age of SIX
A magic wand and box of tricks

At the age of SEVEN
A racing car, battery-driven

At the age of EIGHT
A surfboard, wouldn't that be great?

At the age of NINE
A fishing-rod with reel and line

At the age of TEN
A diary and a fountain pen

What I Got

At the age of ONE
A brick with "RATTLE" painted on

At the age of TWO
A piece of fur and a stick of glue

At the age of THREE
A pair of pram wheels nailed to a tree

At the age of FOUR
A plastic lobster with only one claw

At the age of FIVE
Tickets for the circus (Yet to arrive)

At the age of SIX
One of Granny's hockey sticks

At the age of SEVEN
A stick of rock from Torquay, Devon

At the age of EIGHT
A swimming-ring that wouldn't inflate

At the age of NINE
A safety pin and a ball of twine

At the age of TEN
Dad won the lottery. Bought me Hamleys.

Roger McGough

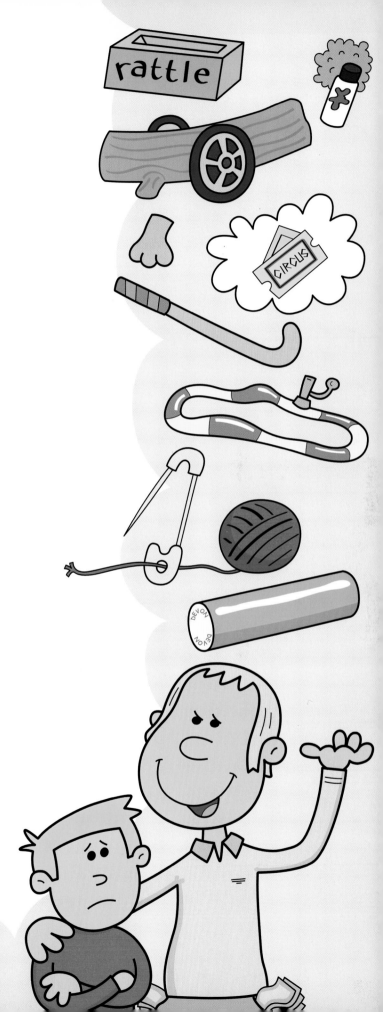

In This Magic Stuff

In this magic stuff there are unmade cars
In this magic stuff there are unformed stars
In this magic stuff – unborn lambs and foals
In this magic stuff – unshapen plates and bowls
In this magic stuff are unbloomed flowers
In this magic stuff there is play for hours
In this magic stuff's what your fancy takes –
In this magic stuff, though, kids first find snakes!

Philip Waddell

This magic stuff is Plasticine

Abracadabra

When somebody gave me a magic kit,
I thought I'd instantly master it.

I thought that rabbits would jump from hats,
I thought my pockets would swarm with rats.

I thought that sparkling lights would shine,
I thought the aces would all be mine.

I thought I'd suddenly disappear,
I thought that people would gasp and cheer.

But now I think that my kit is bust –
Or somebody's stolen my magic dust.

Clare Bevan

Double Ball

Double ball,
double ball,
bounce them off
the playground wall,
under,
over,
through my legs
stuck out stiffly like clothes pegs,
throw them up to touch the sun,
catch them blind – my eyesight's gone!
Grab them! Grapple! Fumble! Flip!
Both of them gave me the slip.

Double Ball

Double ball,
double ball,
bounce them off
the playground wall,
under,
over,
through my legs
stuck out stiffly like clothes pegs,
throw them up to touch the sun,
catch them blind – my eyesight's gone!
Grab them! Grapple! Fumble! Flip!
Both of them gave me the slip.

Gina Douthwaite

The Toy Breaker

I lost bits from my jigsaw
When I threw it on the floor.
And my football, since I stabbed it,
Doesn't blow up any more.

My car I left out in the rain,
(Its battery's gone dead).
I hit my toy clown with a stick,
And now he's lost his head.

I stamped upon my tambourine,
To see if it would break.
It doesn't make a sound these days,
However hard you shake.

It's not my fault at all, you know,
It's just, (as you can tell),
The people who make all these toys
Don't make them very well.

Barry On

Second-hand Toys

I'm the youngest in the family
I'm the smallest in the line
I always get the hand-downs –
I get them all the time.

I got my cousin's Action Man
(the one without a head)
his jigsaw missing pieces
and his broken clockwork Ted.

I got my sister's farmyard
I got her cows and goats
her sailor, with the parrot –
and half the sailor's boat.

My mother calls it sharing...
She says it's nice to do
But I prefer things different
for I prefer things NEW!

Peter Dixon

Dear Father Christmas

Dear Father Christmas,
Please may I have a...

    ...Telescopic, silver-plated
    Electronically created
    Death-ray sting and spurting belly
    Looks disgusting on the telly
    Glow-bright ears, revolving face
    Seven gears with blast-off base
    Extra knee sprays toxic fluid
    (B2 battery not included)
    Ultrasonic, everlasting
    Supertronic, megablasting
    Mad and mighty Monstermort!

    Oh – and marbles, any sort.

Dear Father Christmas,
Thank you for my presents,
        especially the...

    ...Super-slamming, eyeball-smashing
    Whizzing, whamming, baddie-bashing
    Hard as nails, heavyweight
    Bag of marbles. They were great!

    Monstermort, by the way
    Fell apart on Boxing Day.

Jan Burchett and Sara Vogler

Gone

I had it today
For just an hour,
Then, tugged away
By the wind's power
It sailed off free
Above the crowd,
High as a tree,
High as a cloud,
High as the moon,
High as the sun,
My new balloon
Has gone, gone, gone.

Eric Finney

Growing Up

My mum says I've grown out of
my 'superhero' stuff –
my cape's too short for flying,
my tights aren't long enough.

My 'S' for 'superhero'
is stretched all out of shape –
the sleeves squeeze at my elbows,
my mask's held on by tape.

If only it was bigger,
I love my 'hero' kit –
it's just that it's grown too small for me,
I've not grown out of it!

Liz Brownlee

The Sand-snake

Out of a sack
like a snake uncoiling
hissing and slithering
sand pours down
on my red plastic
brand-new sandpit.

If I pour water
brightly bubbling
to make an ocean
the greedy sand-snake
gulps it to nothing
no matter how often
I run to the tap
with my watering-can.

I make a town
of sand houses
and when I'm tired
the sand-snake buries them.
We start again.

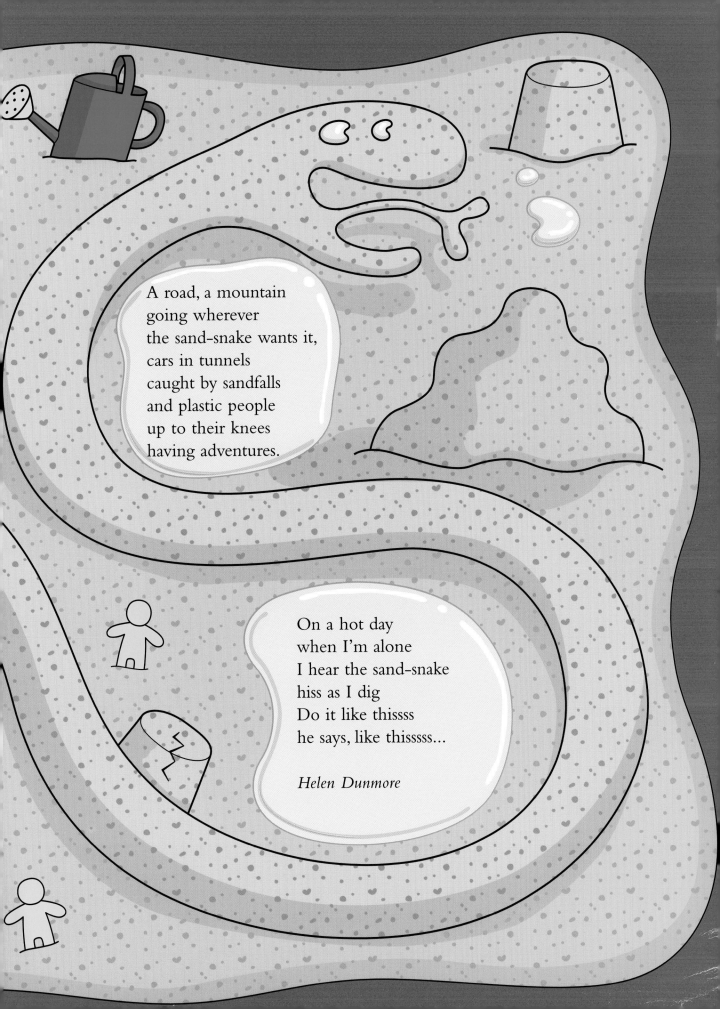

A road, a mountain
going wherever
the sand-snake wants it,
cars in tunnels
caught by sandfalls
and plastic people
up to their knees
having adventures.

On a hot day
when I'm alone
I hear the sand-snake
hiss as I dig
Do it like thissss
he says, like thisssss...

Helen Dunmore

In My Bath

In my bath is
a rubber duck
a bear with one ear
a bit of muck
wooden lorries
a plastic frog
a blob of soap
a woolly dog
my dinner dish
some odd red stuff
a bobbing boat
a ball of fluff
a squeezy bottle
a soggy pea
a lot of water
a lot of water
and
me.

Dave Calder

The Land of Counterpane

When I was sick and lay abed,
I had two pillows at my head,
And all my toys beside me lay
To keep me happy all the day.

And sometimes for an hour or so,
I watched my leaden soldiers go,
With different uniforms and drills,
Among the bedclothes, through the hills;

And sometimes sent my ships in fleets
All up and down among the sheets;
Or brought my trees and houses out,
And planted cities all about.

I was the giant great and still
That sits upon the pillow-hill,
And sees before him, dale and plain,
The pleasant land of counterpane.

Robert Louis Stevenson

The Toys' Playtime

When we go to bed at the end of the day,
our toys wake up and start to play.

They wait until we're fast asleep,
then they come alive and out they creep.

The ball goes bouncing. The doll does a dance.
The little ponies preen and prance.

The toy car roars across the room.
The rocket starts to take off: ZOOM!

The robot reads a picture book,
then Teddy comes and takes a look.

And all the time we're sleeping tight,
the toys are playing through the night.

But when the sunlight warms our faces,
the toys sit quietly in their places.

They do not move. They make no noise.
You don't fool us, you naughty toys!

Tony Mitton

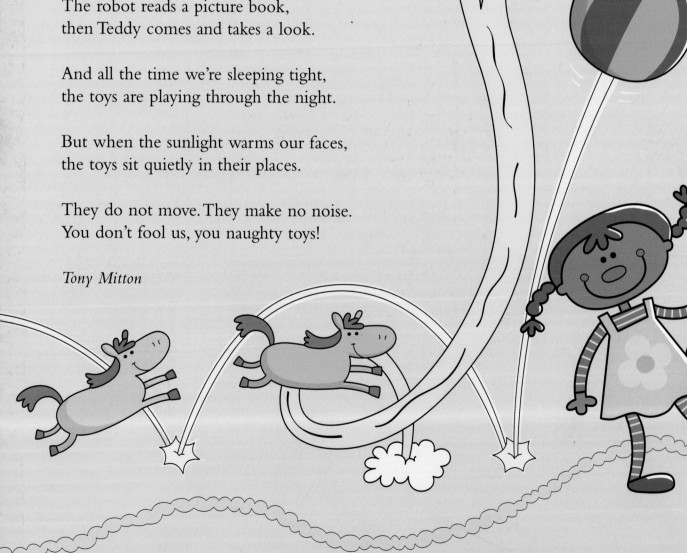